Networking
for
Business Success

QUICK TIPS FOR BUSY PEOPLE

To Peter
All the very best
Heather
15/12/9

Networking
for
Business Success

by

Heather White

**Networking for
Business Success**
Quick Tips for Busy People

© Heather White 2004
www.magicofnetworking.co.uk

First published in Great Britain 2004
Revised edition 2006

ISBN 1904623204

Designed by
e-BookServices.com

Cover design
Studio Projects

This booklet is dedicated to my mum and dad
whom I love with all my heart and soul.
My sincere thanks go to the following people,
as without their help and support this booklet
would have remained"pie in the sky".

So thank you
Ian Rowland, Marion Royer, Michael Vincent, Karen Branco,
Maggie Jackson, Joe Branco, Niki Branco, Lynne Clark, the staff at
London Chamber of Commerce and Industry, Dorne Sowerby,
Neil Kirby, Simon le Jeune, Nadine Chorn, Ian Redington, Jane Couling,
Simon O'Brien, Fergus Lawson, Paul Roberts, Peter Baxter-Derrington,
Steve Connelly, Gordon Jones, Simon Sperryn, Alan Mackelworth
and Christine Lawrence.

I have met every person mentioned above as a result of "networking"
and if I had to pick only one benefit that flows from networking, then
it would be the lifelong friends you make along the way.

Contents

Introduction

Like you I am looking for new business, career development, knowledge, innovation and fulfilment. I use networking as my primary tool to find all these things. Most of my networking takes place on a face-to-face basis with the additional support of emails, letters, articles and telephone calls.

This collection of "nuggets" is based on my own experience as well as the experience of hundreds of professionals from all walks of life and in all sectors. I have attended as many forums as there are sectors, and most of them several times – so each nugget has been tested and re-tested to make sure that it works, and works well.

Here is the good news: effective networkers say that 90% of their new business is generated through proactive networking and word-of-mouth referrals. Outplacement consultancies say that over 70% of new positions in corporations are successfully filled using positive networking strategies. Futurologists rate strategic networking skills and knowledge management at both the enterprise and the individual level as essential skills for the 21st century.

When I first tried it out in London in 1999, I was not a very successful networker and I was very frustrated to be told by other professionals just how powerful networking was when my own efforts were so disappointing. So I decided to find someone who could teach me the skills I needed and use as a role model. But I couldn't find anyone so I worked it out the hard way. I watched other people at networking events, then practised and tested my own approach. I was determined to become one of the world's best networkers! Whilst I am not claiming to have reached that goal yet, my business and personal growth have gone from strength to strength. I realised early on that in order for networking to be effective, strategic planning, practical application and people skills needed to be combined in equal measure. If these elements were not in harmony, results took much longer, or simply didn't materialize.

My friends and fellow professionals noticed how dramatically my business was growing and persuaded me to teach them to network for business success. Teaching networking skills, behaviours and strategies quickly became my passion, and so a new business *"The Magic of Networking"* was born.

The assumption that business people know – or should know – how to network, is very far from the truth: networking is as much a skill as any other managerial competence, but very few people receive any training. When I am asked to run a training programme my brief at the outset is usually to focus on strategy, but the emphasis quickly shifts to improvement of soft skills during the workshop itself. You cannot have one without the other because people buy from people. First they buy you; through you they buy trust, and finally they buy your product or service. If you don't fully understand the concept of networking, are unfamiliar with the process, and uncomfortable in the environment, then networking is not going to work for you unless and until these barriers are removed.

Having been the other side of the barriers myself, nothing gives me greater pleasure now than showing people how strategic networking can help win new business, increase market share, build strategic alliances, increase profile and influence, and fast-track career development.

This book is dedicated to all aspiring networkers, whether enthusiastic (because you want to have a go) or hesitant (because you're being forced into it). I have tried to position the contents so that they will help you to review your objectives, be more analytical about your achievements, and ultimately generate results that you might not have thought were possible.

How to gain the most from this book

This booklet has been designed for busy people looking for quick hints and tips, and so is necessarily brief and to the point. Scanning the contents page will enable you to get straight to your most pressing networking questions.

It deals with the basics. Use the tips for guidance only; it is up to you to develop them in accordance with your own style and situation.

The main objective of this book is to help you gain confidence and acquire the courage to go that bit further.

As one networker to another, I wish you every success. I hope that you have lots of fun discovering 'the magic of networking'!

What networking is (and what is *not*)

Before we get started on the practical hints and tips let's define what I mean by 'networking'.

There are many definitions, most of which are variants on 'developing long-term relationships for mutual gain'. This is a good definition, but I would take it a stage further. For me, networking is about creating residual energy with people so that *your* name springs to mind when a beneficial opportunity arises. Residual energy is what you leave behind after you meet a person, and you do this by creating an impact and building rapport and trust.

The good news is that these skills can be learned and improved upon.

It is important that you also understand the difference between 'doing networking' and being a **'professional networker'**.

Someone who goes out 'hungry', with little thought for the needs of anyone else, is only **doing** networking. Often these people will only get back in contact when they want something. Someone who wants to develop long-term relationships for mutual gain and who is prepared to work at the relationship is a **professional networke**r. These contacts often become genuine friends.

What makes the difference? The holistic nature of the relationship is what makes the difference.

A **professional networker** is unselfish, whereas someone who is "doing" networking – going through the motions – has a selfish agenda.

Something else to bear in mind is that most people would not use the term networking at all. They are simply attending events to gather knowledge or intelligence from the speaker. Many enjoy circulating and seeing what is happening.

My intention is to help you become a **professional networker**.

For me, professional networking is proactive self-marketing to the benefit of all. It means taking action, being very practical and developing an acute sense of what the other person needs. It is about friendship, trust and good old fashioned respect and regard for others.

Networking works, and it works better for learning how to be good at it: a professional approach pays dividends. HOWEVER it works in mysterious ways. For instance, if you are looking for another job you can be 70% sure you will find it through networking but you can never be 100% certain which event, telephone call, conversation or contact is going to lead you to that job. However consciously we manage our networking, it is speculative, and accepting the lack of structure is a key lesson.

At this point you may be feeling that networking is probably a waste of time – which it is not – but it can certainly seem like an act of faith! The trick is to have confidence and patience, knowing that all the time 'wasted' will eventually lead to the result you want.

If we agree on what networking is, then we can easily establish what it is not. Networking is NOT selling. Networking creates an environment in which the intangible pre-sales criteria may be satisfied, and so sets the scene for a sale to take place.

A big mistake people make is to behave the same way with all people and in all situations. It is important to adapt your approach. The saying 'when in Rome do as the Romans do' will serve you well when networking. If you come on too strong, you will turn people off. A typical example when people can come across too strong is when they only start networking in their hour of need: when they need to find a new job quickly, or are desperate for new business. Be careful not to show your hunger!

Remember, your only objective when meeting someone for the first time is to get to know him or her, build the relationship, and find the common ground. If you hit all these buttons there's a good chance a productive networking relationship will develop.

The Networker's Timeline

Four elements determine the speed of your networking success.

1. Time
2. Commitment
3. Attitude
4. Courage

Here is how it works. You need to commit time to build and sustain a proper network. You need to have the right attitude towards networking. Some people need courage to get started. Others will need courage to take more 'emotional' risks. Your objective is to build confidence through experience. As you become more experienced you learn how to add value. As you add more value your reputation will grow, you leave "positive residual enegy" behind, and effective networking will be the result.

People like confident people. They sense that these people are able to deliver and take them closer to their own objectives.

With experience you learn how you can add value to your network. This means standing in the shoes of the other person as well as your own. How you add value is unique to you, but here are a few pointers:

- Become an expert in your field (or be an excellent generalist)
- Get to know what's important to your contacts – understand their business issues
- Develop a diverse and complementary network of contacts
- Introduce your contacts to useful and trustworthy people

Confidence alone is not a guarantee that networking will be successful. Let's take 150 unemployed senior executives I recently worked with. Most said that with the benefit of hindsight they would have networked more. Most agreed they had a large number of contacts in place but did little to nurture these relationships. They needed **quality** not **quantity**. They had not put any work into keeping in touch and developing their networks, so had no support when that rainy day arrived.

When we become unemployed or start our own business we lose something very important: a name with leverage; the company name. Therefore it is vital you build a reputation for excellence – your personal brand - *before* you leave. This takes time, and time is the last thing you will have on your hands when you're in need. So start now and never stop.

The business case for strategic networking

Here is what 70 MBA students from Kingston University Business School said networking can do or be:

- Open career doors
- A better use of time
- Help to make an informed decision
- An 'insurance policy'
- An opportunity to develop personal skills
- Extend personal resources
- A way of gaining industry knowledge
- A way of monitoring competitor activity
- A way of influencing key people
- Bring in new business
- A means of creating a strong, virtual team
- Help develop self-marketing skills
- Help find new employees
- A way of finding new ideas by listening to people
- A way to demonstrate abilities
- A forum where one can test out ideas and skills
- A way of creating a higher profile for oneself
- A forum to support colleagues and clients
- A means of developing your business
- A way to benchmark and exchange best practice
- A way of testing efficiency
- A shortcut to business or personal goals

10

Networking without focus: the pitfalls

If you start with the wrong approach to networking, as I did, you will end up with disappointing results and negative experiences. But in truth nothing is actually wasted, and many of my earlier mistakes - or so I thought - are now bearing fruit in ways that I had never expected.

So what are the pitfalls that we need to be aware of? I asked the same group of MBA students what might be counter-productive about networking and this is what they said. The point I want to make here is 'forewarned is forearmed and could be fore planned … if you want it to be!':

- It can take a lot of time to get started
- You need to be careful about confidentiality
- You can meet the 'wrong' contacts
- Some events have distinct 'in-house cliques'
- It can be difficult to get close to key people
- It may take a long time to start seeing results
- It might be difficult to justify the time to the boss
- You may not get the results you want
- Employees who are successful at networking may end up being poached
- It is easy to lose focus at events
- You can lose impartiality
- Down time away from the desk!

- Effect can be difficult to measure
- There are plenty of blind alleys to lose your way in.

All of these disadvantages can easily be overcome by clarifying your networking objectives, and this book is filled with tips on how to do this. Page 17 will guide you through objective setting.

But in truth, nothing is actually wasted...

So what actually works?

The question I am most often asked is 'Heather, what is the fastest way to get results?'

Overleaf is a checklist of issues you need to think about and put in place. This does take time but if networking is how business comes to you then what else is there to do? Networking is as much a process as other forms of marketing.

What also speeds up the results is being clear about why you bother. I hate cold calling, and I find mail shots can be expensive and a waste of time. On the other hand, I love meeting people and I learn best through discussion and observation; plus I achieve better results on a one-to-one basis. So the reason I network is because I want to meet a person/company who may not otherwise take my telephone call or reply to my letters, in order to develop a long-term relationship with them.

What works is having a motivating reason for doing it, so what is yours?

My reason for networking is…

....

....

....

....

....

13

The fast path to networking success is as follows:

Right people

- Be clear who you want to meet.
- It is easier if you like this person.
- Find willing connectors, specialists and influencers (read *the Tipping Point* by Malcolm Gladwell for more clues on this - very, very powerful).

Right place

- Attend events where you will find large clusters of the types of people you want to meet (see pages 23,25,26,28,29,30).
- Do a mixture of attending events and one-to-one meetings.

Right event organisers

- Someone is organising an event for the people you want to meet so get onto their mailing list.
- Find these organisers by searching the web.

Mind set

- Having met the right people, your mind set should be that they will be in your life for a very long time.

Personal and business brand - message

- Get clear about your person and business message. For example I want people to remember this: "Networking .... you need Magic".
- Walk your talk - people will spot incongruence in a second.

Soft skills, people skills, communication skills

- Keep one thing in mind - stay focused on building trust and rapport.
- Develop respect and understanding.
- Get into their shoes - and use them.
- Learn their language - and use it.
- If I don't click with them, introduce to a colleague.
- If my colleague doesn't click with them - walk away and try again another time.
- Think all the time - "how can I add value to my contacts".

Business and marketing objectives

- Align your networking activity to your business and marketing objectives.
- Build a team strategy and then break down how the individuals are going to approach this.

Buying cycles and cultures

- Align your networking activities and approach to that of the normal buying cycle of your clients - understand what triggers people buying from you or your type of services.

Staying in touch

- You should spend more time/focus on staying in touch with existing good/right contacts than going out and finding more new people.
- How you stay in touch should obviously align with your contacts buying cycle as well.

- It is so much easier to stay in touch with someone you like - the effort is less and it feels great. In my experience that's when the unexpected happens - a bit like Magic really.
- Most importantly staying in touch with a person does NOT guarantee a return on investment - it doesn't work like that. See it as what goes around comes around.

Commitment and consistency

- Being clear about the benefits of networking for you and your business
- Being committed to making it work

Time wasters

The opposite of everything on the list above - plus a few extra thoughts.

- If they are not willing, no matter how able or right - it won't happen - find someone else.
- All your eggs in one basket or too few contacts.
- Everyone pouncing on the same few contacts.
- Having a massive contact list and doing nothing with it.
- Just sending out a new brochure or email every 6 months say "buy from me".
- Forever finding new contacts.
- Scattergun approach - rarely works.

Your networking objectives

One reason why people do not achieve the results they want from networking is because they are not clear about their reasons for networking. In the course of my own work with individuals or corporate teams, I always start with an audit. It might help you if you did the same to clarify your own objectives. The Magic of Networking Audit can be downloaded from www.magicofnetworking.co.uk.

The main benefit you will get from taking time out to do this is that once you are clear about your reasons for networking, you will have a better idea of how and where to network for results.

What this means in practice is that, if you are networking because you want to improve your profile or your soft skills, your approach will be very different from, say networking to develop new business.

How you network also means taking into account *who* you want to network with. Remembering that networking is not selling but by speaking to a person you may create an opportunity. This is when you start the knock-on effect. *How* you network depends upon *who* you are networking with and your objectives.

Case study 1

Let's take two simple case studies to help you think through your own situation :

Person A is a financial director. She wants to change jobs in the next 12 months. She is considering moving from insurance to healthcare. She also wants to move from London to Kent. Her strength is that she is in no hurry, but she needs to be careful that she does not lose momentum if she is going to be successful.

It would be a good idea for her to attend events for financial directors organised by, for example, The Institute of Chartered Accountants (www.icaew. co.uk) to find financial directors working within the healthcare sector. Her objective would be to develop relationships with them in order to learn more about the healthcare sector. She could support her networking activities with information about potential employers in Kent, using the internet, local authorities, or the British Library.

It would also be a good idea to track down the relevant industry associations and start attending London events to become familiar with topical issues. Possible sources of help might be The Local Government Association (www.lga.gov.uk) or The NHS Alliance (www.nhsalliance.org). She needs to start raising her profile in this sector now, because there can be resistance to recruiting people from outside. One way of doing this is to start reading relevant trade magazines and commenting on the hot topics via letters or articles.

Depending on whether she wants to work with an established business or a start-up, she might also consider networking at events for venture capitalists (www.bvca.co.uk).

Her main objective is to build relationships with people to the point where they immediately think about her when an opportunity arises even though she is not with them. Therefore she also has to devise a system that ensures she stays in touch regularly.

Activity, relationships and results should be reviewed after about six months, at which point it might be a good idea to start talking to headhunters and specialist recruitment agencies – never forgetting that 70% of senior positions are filled through word of mouth.

In summary she is networking on three levels:

1. Learning and understanding the market.
2. Developing relationships with intermediaries.
3. Raising her profile to employers in the sector.

Case study 2

Person B is a self-employed headhunter. He wants to grow his business and be known in the market as the headhunter of second choice. He knows that businesses often become dissatisfied with the first headhunter when they don't deliver on their promise. He is in a fiercely competitive market. He wants to profile his business within the telecommunications and technology sectors.

His buyers have a love/hate relationship with head-hunters, so he has to be perceived differently. Therefore his main purpose in networking is to add value to his contacts, not to sell.

He should select business forums attended by future buyers and future candidates. Candidates eventually become buyers. He needs to build trust and rapport with these people. Often this is best achieved by making a contribution to the sector.

He will be networking to gain market information so that he can contribute his own opinion, introduce a wider perspective, and demonstrate this knowledge to those he needs to influence. He can also add value to his contacts by signposting them to other useful suppliers who can themselves add value. (Don't forget that people are always looking for good contacts to help save them time).

In fact, this person did achieve his objective of growing his business by establishing a reputation as the "headhunter of second choice". He did this exactly as described, by networking for information about the sector and then bringing new ideas and approaches to the notice of the influencers with whom he networked to develop relationships. New business followed as a result, and all through the power of networking.

How to get started

Write down your networking objectives. You may have different objectives for different situations, but the first step is to clarify them. So for example, how many objectives you need to tick from the list below.

- Sell your products/services?
- Change career?
- Change sector?
- Improve career opportunities?
- Gain market information?
- Learn something?
- Test something?
- Make the first contact with a particular person?
- Set up an appointment with a particular person?
- Have a conversation with a particular person?
- Establish rapport with a particular person?
- Cement a relationship?
- Listen, and check out a situation?
- Find competitors and see what they are doing?
- Introduce your contact(s) to this forum?
- Find people to fill the gaps in your own networks?
- Develop a relationship with a client/colleague?
- Improve your profile?
- Meet a speaker?
- Have some fun?
- Just find out what is going on "out there"?

Make a list of your objectives

My networking objectives:

....

....

....

....

....

....

....

....

....

....

....

....

....

....

....

....

....

....

....

....

....

....

....

....

Who do you want to meet?

The most common mistake business people make is to attend events that do not lead them to the right people in the right circumstances. When I am invited to a networking event the first question I ask myself is *'Are the people I want to meet going to be attending this event?'* Whilst other factors also influence my decision, my principle is to go where my potential contacts go.

So, who do you want to meet? Transfer your answer onto the next page.

- Large organisations?
- Small organisations?
- Start-ups?
- Mature businesses?
- Private sector?
- Public sector?
- Not-for-profits/charities?
- Business services?
- Suppliers?
- Independent professionals?
- Employees?
- A particular company?
- A particular person, such as the speaker, the sponsors?
- Gender-specific or minority ethnic groups?
- Functional heads such as CEO, HR, Marketing, etc?

Who do you want to influence?

If you want to influence particular people – whether inside or outside your organisation - it is important to make a list and jot down a few things to consider:

- Their names and functions.
- The names of the people who influence them.
- What are they likely to be influenced by?
- What is important to them?
- Understand their personality type.

In following your strategy make sure you always deliver, and never confuse sycophancy with influencing!

People and organisations I want to meet:

....

....

....

....

....

....

....

....

....

....

....

....

How to stack networks

Over time I realised that my networks had themes, and the more I worked the common ground the easier networking became. It became easier because I was able to effectively link people within my networks with each other.

It is notable that most people attend events organised for their peer groups. For example, rarely would I meet an HR person at an event for the industry they work in; they would be at an event for HR peer groups. Neither would I find a CEO at an HR event.

Your networking should take you in and out of many different networks to achieve your objectives.

People tend to cluster around the following themes:

- Peer groups
- Industry groups
- Subject matter
- Geographical areas
- Gender or ethnic issues

Themes that can attract a mixed group of people would include:

- Art
- Sports
- Causes

- Charities
- Famous speakers

Your networking should take you in and out of many different networks to achieve your objectives.

Example:

You are a Financial Director in transition. You want to meet CEOs within the mobile phone industry, preferably start-up businesses, with a European focus. The groups you might consider networking within would include:

- A Sector-based groups, i.e. Telecommunications Executive Network (www.gateway10.com)
- CEO level groups, i.e. Institute of Directors (www.iod.co.uk) - wide range of CEOs however
- FD level groups, i.e. Institute of Chartered Accountants (www.icaew.co.uk)
- Groups for new or expanding businesses, i.e. British Venture Capital Association (www.bvca.co.uk)
- Groups with a European focus, i.e. Federation of Telecoms or Engineers of the European Community (www.fitce.org)
- High level generalist groups, i.e. The Executive Network (www.theexecutivenetwork.com)

Within any of these forums, keep an eye out for special interests groups which run separate events alongside the main event.

How often should I be 'out' networking?

This section is a general guide only, as business backgrounds and objectives will vary quite considerably. It is very important to note that it is going to take you at least 6–12 months to build a solid network of contacts. Providing you maintain this level of activity, the time invested will pay dividends for the rest of your life.

- It is important to have at least one face-to-face appointment each week to nurture contacts.
- It is important to attend 'group networking' events at least three times a month.
- It is important to be talking to your top 20% contacts at least every other month, if not more.

How to find the people you want to meet

There are innumerable organisations putting on events for business people. You could spend your whole life just attending events, and it would all be very interesting but probably unproductive! It follows that it can be very frustrating trying to find the *right* event, the one that the people you want to meet are attending. To give yourself the best chance of doing this you need to understand why busy people leave their desks to attend an event. Usually it is a mixture of problems, situations and needs. For example:

- A problem might be solved by attending an event about **employment law**, or
- An event with an **industry focus,** such as banking and finance.
- Some groups draw from a **geographical area**, such as Docklands.
- Others segment by **demographics**, i.e. "Black Women in Business".
- Many groups bring together **functional peers** i.e. CEO, CFOs etc.
- Many others are based around a **common cause**, such as politics, religion or sport.

And yes you are right, we made the same point on page 25. So it is important to understand why your contacts flock to events, therefore making it easy for you to find them.

The first stage is to understand why people make the effort to attend an event. The second stage is to think about who puts on events to attract these very people.

- Business groups.
- Membership organisations.
- Providers of products and services.
- Event organisers (conferences and exhibitions).
- Trade and professional associations (federations, institutes).
- Special interest groups (there are many of these inside membership organisations).

How does knowing all this help you?

- If you want to parachute right into a group of people you want to meet, you need to know where they are gathering and who is putting on the event for them.
- *Where* you network will determine *how* you network, i.e. you will take different approaches when attending a client event, an event for the industry sector, a conference, a seminar, etc.

How to find the people you want to meet

How to select membership organisations to meet your objectives

- Always make an appointment to meet someone from the membership organisation.
- Always attend at least 2-3 events before signing up.
- Make a point of meeting a few longstanding members.
- Ask for a full list of services provided by the organisation.
- Find out if there is a members' meeting point.
- Find out if there is a business library.
- Find out if membership covers overseas clubs.
- Find out how members are introduced to each other.
- Ask for the membership profile and determine if it is aligned to your business objectives.
- Think about how you could contribute to the aims of the organisation – it's a two-way relationship.

How to move from one sector to another

- Review some of the points made in the preceding sections.
- Find trade magazines that promote events.
- List any existing contacts you already have in the field you want to move into.
- Network with people in your organisation who might already be involved in the new sector.
- List the top 10 businesses in that sector, call the marketing departments and get on their mailing list.
- Don't forget to use the internet for additional background.
- Go along to an event to pick up information, ask questions and listen to the answers carefully.
- Formulate a plan based on the networking style of the sector.

How to work a room

Although I dislike the expression 'work a room' because it sounds clinical and selfish, it does neatly explain what this section covers. It is also what most people want to know more about. I cannot emphasis enough that attending events is just one part of a networker's activity plan.

Over the years I have found one-to-one meetings are more productive than just going to events.

When I do attend an event it is because I want to:

- Meet particular people who otherwise would be difficult to meet.
- Listen to a speaker.
- Gather intelligence.
- Test new material.
- Test how effective I am at developing rapport.
- Profile my business.

Building trust and rapport

Remember the golden rule of networking: build trust and rapport so that people think of you when an opportunity arises. That means forsaking the short-term benefit in favour of the long-term relationship.

- You are not there to sell (though there are a few exceptions to this rule).
- You are there to find and develop contacts.
- Relax and enjoy yourself!
- Build the conversation based on common ground.
- Show genuine interest.
- Learn how to read body language.
- Listen and learn how a person prefers to communicate.
- Stay engaged throughout the conversation.
- Develop the conversation.

OK, so there are no details on how to do any of the above points. However, if you follow the principles and magically trust, rapport will happen. If it does not then consider:

1. You are not engaging in the process
2. You are still focused on yourself
3. They can't see the connection with you

So try a different approach. Try again and again until it drops into place.

Remember the golden rule of networking: build trust and rapport so that people think of you when an opportunity arises. That means forsaking the short-term benefit in favour of the long-term relationship.

How to get over the fear of sounding or looking stupid

Remember, right at the start of this book I mentioned confidence and courage. Now is the time when you will need both. Sounding stupid is a major concern for most people: it certainly was for me. As I met more and more influential people, I learned to be more relaxed about what I said and did. The following have worked very well for me – why don't you try a few?

- If it is a new situation for you, ask questions and listen carefully, but do join in.
- If you are talking to a really important person, ask questions and listen more, but do join in.
- If you are in a group of people, let others do the talking until you are comfortable, but do join in.
- Practise your skills on people you are unlikely to do business with, and watch their response.
- If you don't get the response you want, try again and again and again.
- Practise your body language, introductions, questions, and conversation development.
- Purposely move out of your comfort zone.
- Place yourself intentionally in difficult conversations and learn to feel relaxed about it.

The more you do of this, the less you will feel stupid – I promise!

What to do when you first arrive

- Think briefly about your objectives - even if you just want to have some fun!

- Put your briefcase and other accessories into the cloak room.

- Buy a very good business-card holder in advance, and place about 12 business cards in your pocket.

- Never dish out your cards willy-nilly as you will lose respect.

- Pin your name badge on the top right of your jacket so it is easy to see and read – yes, men, this includes you!

- Introduce yourself to the sponsors/organisers and find out about their objectives and focus.

- Do some "kitchen networking" to warm up, that is, go to the refreshment area and have a drink or some food (but not both at the same time).

- Start a conversation with someone around the food and drinks area if you want an "easy in".

- Read the guest list if there is one, and highlight anyone you want to meet.

- Watch the room and see what is happening, who is talking to who, who is alone.

- Learn to feel comfortable standing on your own and don't make a move too quickly.

How to find your 'needle in a haystack'

If you don't know what your contact looks like or you have not pre-arranged to meet, try some of the following approaches:

- Check with reception to see if the person has arrived.
- If they have not arrived, ask the organiser/ receptionist to find you when they do.
- Always wear something distinctive to help people to find you.
- Ask the organiser/receptionist if they can remember what the person looks like.
- Ask the organiser/receptionist if they would introduce you.
- If the organiser/receptionist doesn't know what the person looks like, return to the room, go up to the first group in the room that looks welcoming, and interrupt their conversation in a friendly way.
- Ask the group if they know the person you are looking for.
- If they do not, ask them if they would mention you if they come across this person.
- Make a new approach to a new group, and do so with humour and honesty.
- Have fun with this approach and the groups will love you for it.
- Keep on until you succeed: you will find your contact within six hits!

If you are unhappy breaking into groups try some of the following - they really work.

How to break into a group of strangers

- Before breaking into a group, assess the intensity of the conversation and body language.

- If it is intense do not break into this group.

- If you need to meet a certain person in that group, stand to one side and wait till the intensity dies down before joining them.

If eye contact is not intense try the following:

- Move towards the group and make clear eye contact with one person.

- Move into the group and ensure your body language is open.

- Do not interrupt the flow of the conversation verbally unless invited.

- Join in by using your facial expression and body language.

- Don't shake hands at this stage unless invited to do so.

- Do participate in the conversation when you can add value.

- Don't just stand there waiting to be asked about yourself.

How to get settled into a new group easily

- Say your first name clearly so that people don't have to strain to hear.

- If you have an unusual name, provide a 'hook' so that people can remember it easily.

- When shaking hands with people in a group do so slowly. Don't rush the encounter.

- When the person says their name, repeat it back to them. Concentrate hard and listen carefully.

- If you don't hear the name clearly ask for it to be repeated. Concentrate and listen.

- Stay enthusiastic, alert and interested. If you aren't, why should they be interested in you?

- Find common ground to connect quickly.

- Have a list of questions in your mind to stimulate the conversation.

The 'glazed look'
(and what you can do about it)

- As soon as you see someone glazing over, take stock of what you are talking about in relation to that person.

- Very quickly bring that particular line of conversation to a close and ask a question to re-engage them.

- It works for me if I re-engage people with a little humour and some cheekiness!

- Sometimes I allow a silence to occur. The 'glazed look' might simply mean that the person is thinking about what I have just said. (Serious people do this a lot).

- If I decide that the person I am talking to is not interested in what we are talking about after all - even though they may have initiated the conversation – I would normally thank them for their time and let them move on.

What do you say when they ask you "What do you do?"

Without wishing to cause offence, it is clear that a response such as "accountant", "financial adviser", or "web designer" is enough to kill some conversations stone dead. The same can be said of other professions such as law, consultancy, training, business support/ advice and so on. In many cases we are our own worst enemies, as we talk about what we do with the same level of passion as watching paint dry! You can fix this little problem with a better understanding of what might be happening during this brief exchange.

- When you say what you do, the other person makes a split-second decision about what they think you are trying to sell them, and whether they want that product/service or not. If they don't they will simply turn off.

- If they have attended the event to find buyers, they might also make a split-second judgement that you are unlikely to buy anything from them.

- If you have not shown any passion or excitement about what you do, it is difficult for them to show interest.

- If your line of work is stereotyped with a boring, ruthless or hard-sell image, they are responding to the stereotype. You might need to try describing what you do in a different way.

For example:

- Not a 'physiotherapist' but a 'physical mentor specialising in backs and sports injuries'.
- Not a 'chartered accountant' but a 'specialist in business tax avoidance'.
- Not an 'independent financial adviser' (IFA) but a 'wealth creator specialising in high-income earners'.
- Not a 'trainer' but a 'facilitator of partnership development'.
- Not a 'web designer' but a 'visual marketing executive specialising in small business growth'.
- Not a 'printer' but a 'print cost containment adviser'.

So, if you usually get a less-than-enthusiastic response when you tell people what you do:

- The other person is relating your words to their last experience, which might not be a positive one.
- Ask the other person to introduce themselves first so that you can pitch your own introduction at a level of interest to them.
- Test out other titles and see how people respond.
- Constantly look for the hooks and test different approaches.

Creating the conversation

Many professionals believe that we should all have a prepared and well rehearsed 60-second' presentation (elevator speech). I would totally agree, but I would also advise only to use this if absolutely necessary. Instead, always drip-feed your experience and knowledge into the conversation as it develops. This is far more natural.

- Talk about yourself with passion and interest, as if it is the first time you've done this.
- Say your first name and your company name slowly as people do not always concentrate.
- Devise several different ways of describing who you are and what you do.
- How you introduce yourself will vary according to your reasons for wanting to meet the person you are speaking to.
- Keep good eye contact throughout.
- Stay alert and sensitive to body language.
- Finish on a question that drives the relationship forward.
- Create a conversation, don't rehearse a script!

Finding common ground

Networking works when opportunities are referred to you by people you have connected with. This can only happen if you have built up trust and rapport. Trust and rapport are built initially during a conversation, so your objective is to find the common ground.

- If possible, ask people to introduce themselves to you first

- Once they have told you who they are and what they do, ask yourself who you know in a similar profession

- Make use of your knowledge about their profession and make a positive statement about it

- Find out why you are both at the same event

- Ask a provocative question about that profession but do not insult the person

- Ask questions to learn more about what they do. So what if you end up asking 100 CEOs what they do. Your concern is about engagement and interest, gaining and developing trust, respect and rapport. There is always something to learn.

- Make sure the tone of your voice is enquiring, even playful!

Why leave a gap in the group?

Whenever you attend an event always observe others. Watch for level of eye contact, closeness of the group, engagement, energy level and the level of intensity. It is best to join a group that is displaying low intensity, one where it is not so animated. Have fun noticing how men and women behave differently!

- People like space; many are not comfortable with close encounters.

- When joining a group, leave a gap to allow others to join in or to leave the group.

- If someone fills the gap, create another one.

- If it happens again, explain to the group what you are doing – enjoy the dance!

Five ways to remember names and faces quickly

Yep, it is that old chestnut! Just how do you remember names and faces? If you are really serious then go and buy a book on this subject. If you are semi-serious then follow these quick tips and you will achieve a reasonable level of success. You see, the reason why you forget names and faces is because you are not concentrating on them!

- Give the person 100% of your attention when they say their name.

- Say the person's name at least three times during the conversation but not like a parrot!

- Don't worry about what you are going to say next; that is why we forget names.

- When you are given a card, look at it carefully and make an association between the person's face and their card.

- If they run their own business, make a positive and genuine comment about their card as this will also anchor the name and card.

- What is important is the intent you have to build a long-term relationship – If it is genuine their name will stick.

What to do if you have forgotten a person's name

- If you are still with them take a quick peek at their name badge (another reason why we should wear badges top right).

- Listen carefully to the conversation as most people's names are mentioned occasionally.

- Say you have misplaced their business card and ask if they have another one.

- If you have their business card with you take a quick look again.

- Once you have their name again, repeat it two or three times to make sure you don't forget.

- Remember: stay focused and it will work for you.

- If all else fails be honest, be sincere, smile and ask them to tell you their name again. People really don't take offence if you ask.

How to give and receive business cards

There are many schools of thought on this subject. They range from giving out your card the minute you meet anyone, to only giving it out when there is enough common ground between two parties and some level of rapport has been established. I sit in the latter school. Anything else to me is selling and being a networking nuisance.

- Only offer your card if you have built some rapport or the other person has shown some interest.

- When you are given a card look at it carefully.

- During or immediately after a conversation make notes on the business card.

- Include comments such as date and place of meeting and relevant key action points.

- Make a note about the category this person fits into for your various projects.

- It is acceptable to offer your card to one person in the group only.

How to leave a group professionally

Tell people why you are leaving. Reasons and mechanisms could include the following:

- 'I'd like to continue circulating. Thank you, it has been most interesting'.
- 'May I introduce you to someone else as I need to carry on circulating?'
- 'I would like to introduce you to X as I think they might be a useful contact'.
- 'This has been very interesting. Thank you'.
- 'There are other people I wish to meet and I appreciate your time'.
- 'I will be in contact with you later this week. Thank you'.
- 'I shall expect your call later. Really looking forward to speaking to you again'.
- 'Please excuse me.'

However…

- Make sure you do not make someone feel rejected or unimportant.
- Shake hands with the person/group, repeating names if appropriate.
- Say how and when you are going to follow up, if you are (letter, email, fax or telephone).
- If you have not done so, give out your card (but, only if appropriate).

Trapped by the network bore?

- First of all, make sure it is not you who is boring!

- Do not destroy a person's self-esteem by making them feel useless and boring.

- To stop a conversation, simply hold out your hand to shake theirs. Like a magnet their hand will come out to yours though they may not understand why.

- Shake their hand and say that you have other people you must meet.

- Offer to introduce them to someone else who might be useful to them.

- Take responsibility for making the conversation interesting.

- Take time to find out what really motivates this person.

Networking isn't working for you? Test the waters!

This subject needs a little explaining. Often when we network we don't always achieve the results we want. This could be due to a number of factors: you might not have made much of an impression; your message might be unclear; you are not adding value; you come across as aloof, or too pushy. Primarily it will be down to your people skills and how you communicate with others, so I have learnt to use networking events to practise my people skills.

Think about it. Here you are in a room with a hundred people. You get the chance to meet, say, ten people over the evening. For each person you meet, your objective is to see how well you keep each person you meet engaged. Select people who either impress or intimidate you in some way. All you have to do is to watch how they respond to you. If you get a negative response, try a different approach. If you get a positive response, develop this approach further. What is great about this is that you get instant feed-back so that you can change your approach immediately. People's body language rarely lies.

At this stage of the book, do I still need to sell the benefits of networking? Networking is a contact sport; it is not a passive activity. For networking to happen, to get people thinking about you positively when an opportunity arises, you have got to make an impact. Therefore, develop your personal profile. Understanding how to make an impact on people is very important.

More benefits: the more you engage with others the more people share with you. The more you understand topics and connections, the more you can add value to your network and to any conversation. The more people find you interesting, the greater your confidence, and so on.

I test my skills and approach whenever I can but one of my favourite places is at networking events. These events allow me to test an approach with, say, four or five different people and get instant feedback.

The feedback I am obviously looking for is one that takes me closer to my objectives, e.g. the appointment, rapport, information, friendship etc. **My one rule however is never to test anything that I believe is going to be to the detriment of another person.**

When I first started to test my skills I was very uncomfortable and concerned. You might be feeling the same right now. A friend reminded me that if I continued to do as I had always done, nothing would change in my life and I would end up with the same results. That was a fair comment.

But what really sold the idea to me was an observation I made when I first started to test my skills. When people met me for the first time they saw only what I presented to them. So if I was clumsy, uncertain, shy, etc., they would only see that. However, if I chose to show confidence, humour and interest they would see that instead.

So I decided that I would only test approaches that helped me look and sound more professional, more helpful, more proficient, more humourous and so on. Where was the harm in that? Why don't you try it out and experience the difference?

- Test your communication styles
- Test new ideas
- Test your body language
- Test your handshake
- Test your introductions
- Test the energy you create in people
- Test your eye contact
- Test stepping out of your comfort zone
- Test how you respond and how others respond to you
- Test different ways of approaching a group, leaving a group, etc
- Attend different groups to see which ones work best for you
- Test yourself on your peer group
- Test to see how soon people lose interest in you and when you get it back again

Networking isn't working for you?
Test the waters!

How to follow up for results

Follow-up is simple - provided you have already established a strong rapport with the person concerned and if there was a clear understanding of how and when you would stay in touch. If neither happened, then follow-up is hard. Here are some simple principles which shows how important it is not to sell on a first meeting, unless it is entirely appropriate.

- Agree with the other person what you are going to do, and do it.

- Agree how you will make contact i.e. email, telephone, letter, etc.

- Do exactly what you said you would do.

- Do something for them which is not related to what you are selling.

- Ask them if they are happy with you putting their details on your database.

- Find out who they want to meet or what other services they are looking to buy, and see if you can signpost them.

What to do with all those business cards

Let me ask you a question. At the moment where do you keep all your business cards? What I see so often is wasted effort. People collect cards, do nothing with them, don't stay in touch but allow the sight of these cards to give them stress. Daft really!

- Create an electronic record system (Access, Excel, ACT! Microsoft Outlook).
- Enter the details from the card at your earliest opportunity.
- Keep the cards, and file in a system that works for you.
- Consider filing cards by what people do, their services, their interests etc.
- You can always ask for extra cards from your contact if that helps you.
- If you don't have time to put then onto your system, find some one who will.

At the end of the day your database is your asset - so taking it serious and being organised is important.

Networkers: they're all so different!

How you 'work a room' should vary according to your reasons for being there, the types of people you are going to meet and the environment that has been created. Treat every individual with respect, as an opportunity to discover something new, to learn something and to enjoy the process.

Consider:

- Businesses of the same size may have nothing in common with each other than their size.

- Employees working in administration will be motivated differently from sales people.

- Directors and management will have different perspectives on the business.

- How these people relate to each other creates interesting dynamics.

- Be sensitive to what 'drives' people: it is normally very easy to spot.

- Remember many people network to 'sell' rather than 'buy', which, as we know, is not networking.

- Remember many people don't attend events to network. People can object to be 'networked' on.

How to deal with rejection

I have been rejected by more people than you would believe possible! The interesting thing is that most people who have 'rejected' me had no idea that I felt rejected!

Why? Two reasons. On the one hand, most people are not aware that I have taken their action personally, and on the other hand, it is unreasonable to expect everyone to like me or my services the first, second or even the third time we meet.

Sometimes we feel rejected because of own feelings of inadequacy. Usually, people will have no idea they triggered these, so we can hardly blame them for not knowing how we feel.

In my experience it is rare to meet someone who is knowingly very rude and rejects you in an unpleasant way. It helps that over the years I have learned to develop a thicker skin and just move on to the next person or topic quickly; you can too!

It might help to consider these points…

- If someone turns their back on you, the chances are they did not see you approaching.
- A person may be so focused on something else they simply do not see you.
- Not being 'allowed' into a group might mean an important conversation needs to be finished first.
- If a person does not want to meet you, they just might be too busy at that moment.
    - Or perhaps they don't see the connection just yet.
    - Or they are not ready to buy just yet.
- To avoid rejection watch body language closely and estimate the state of play.
- To avoid rejection watch your own body language closely as that will steer the conversation.
- If you see someone turn off, close the conversation and create a positive goodbye.
- You can always try again later.
- Don't join groups that are heavily engrossed in conversation or you will be rejected, and quite right too!
- Don't interrupt speakers when a crowd has gathered around them – they are enjoying themselves!

People skills; communication skills; soft skills

Throughout this book you will find constant references to one main principle behind networking success.

People buy from people first.

People are buying trust, professionalism, expertise, "people like me" and so on.

Work on your people skills and treat others as you would want to be treated.

Use respect, appreciation, honesty, transparency, trust, support, consideration, and you will succeed.

Quality questions stimulate quality responses

- Rather than talk just about yourself, ask questions of the other person.
- Talk about what you do only if invited. Don't force your information on others.
- People only listen when they are ready to, so create that opportunity.
- It is quite in order for a conversation to finish without you contributing information about yourself.
- Memorise at least ten good generic questions.
- Be genuine and animated each time you ask a question.
- Listen carefully and frame another question out of the response.
- Be careful not to make the process sound like an inquisition.
- Quality questions should have a strong 'emotional hook' to stimulate the conversation.
- Your face, voice, eyes and body language should express real interest, not just technique.

Concerned you might dry up?
Questions you could try

Your questions should reflect your objective(s) and that of the other person. I try to avoid superficial chitchat unless that is how the other person prefers to establish trust, or the environment I find myself in suits that type of conversation. The questions below are just a guide, and should start you thinking of others. I tend to have about five questions in my mind, just in case I dry up.

Questions relating directly to work:

1. How did you get started as a …? / in your trade?
2. What was your biggest challenge?
3. What brings you here tonight?
4. What did you think of the speaker?
5. What did you learn from tonight?
6. What gave you the idea to …?
7. Where did you study?
8. How long did you have to study for?
9. What do you find is the best way to…?
10. If you could start again, would you do anything differently?
11. Can you recommend a book, trade magazine, exhibition, club, network, etc?
12. Can you offer me any advice/direction on …?
13. What contacts are you looking for?
14. Who are your clients?

15. Why do you attract that type of client?

16. What is your marketing strategy?

17. What is your biggest challenge when trying to bring in new business?

18. What sort of people do you employ?

19. What sort of challenges are you facing at the moment, i.e. skills shortages?

20. Do you have any favourite websites?

21. What do you hate most about IT?

22. What new markets are you thinking of going in to?

23. What level of autonomy do you have?

24. Who do you want to meet?

25. Have you been to one of these events before?

Questions which are more personal, some relating to work and others to the person:

1. What are you most proud of?

2. What was your most embarrassing moment?

3. Where do you go for …?

4. Who are your role models and why?

5. Are you doing anything differently now compared with five years ago?

6. Do you have any hobbies?

7. What started you on that hobby?

8. What motivates you to carry on doing …?

9. How difficult was it to get started?

10. Do you have a 'passion' in life?

11. Where do you want to be in five years' time?

12. How does your job affect you personally?

13. Are you happy in your job?

14. What is your favourite sport?

15. What football team do you support?

16. What is the funniest thing that has ever happened to you at work?

17. What is the scariest thing that has ever happened to you?

18. I have always wanted to know …?

19. I am looking for … Do you know him/her?

If you are table-hosting/networking here are some topics you could introduce:

1. What would you do with an extra room?

2. Who would you absolutely love to have a conversation with?

3. Do you have an unfulfilled dream?

4. What is the scariest thing you have ever done?

5. What sports are you into?

6. Let's make a bet on the length of the speech.

7. What do you hate to be asked?

8. What did you want to be when you were young?

9. Is there anywhere in the world you'd like to travel to?

10. Who would you like to have dinner with?

11. What is your favourite film/theatre/opera etc?

12. What is your favourite holiday destination?

13. Have you been on holiday this year?

14. What do you think of education today?

15. What's your idea of a great day/night out?

16. If you could live anywhere in the world where would it be?

17. What would be the first thing you would buy if you won the lottery?

18. If you didn't have to worry about money, what job in the world would you do, or would you do one?

19. Do you really think there is more crime these days or is there just more reporting?

Know what your body language says

Most professional people I meet say they are fairly aware of other people's body language, yet most are not aware of what they are communicating with their own. I challenge you to take real notice of how you listen, how you stand and the tone of your voice. Before we can start to understand others we need to be fully aware of how others perceive us. So the first stage is to become aware of how you normally listen and express yourself through your own body language. The following points should help you.

- What is your handshake like? It is the first and most important point of contact.
- When you shake hands, do you make good eye contact for a brief second?
- Is your body language consistent with your voice, eyes and hands?
- Are you really listening or just playing "face games"?
- Do you really know what message you are conveying with your body language?
- How would you respond to being introduced to a famous person, or an interesting professional such as a magician, or to an accountant?
- Be delighted to meet everyone, every time, but don't be false.
- Treat everyone with the same respect.

I often see people who are indifferent to one person and then nice to another person simply because they believe they may get something from the latter. Remember there are no 'little people' in this world, only human beings. Everyone has value.

How to establish instant rapport

People skills are judged instantly, so what are yours like?

Think about:

- Your handshake
- Your eye contact
- How confident you appear
- How appropriately you are dressed
- How well you listen
- How well you engage in the conversation
- How you use the conversation to create rapport and understanding
- How focused you remain
- When to leave and when to keep quiet!
- How professionally you present your company, yourself and your knowledge
- If you remember names
- Being considerate to those around you
- Fakes will be detected.

Develop your powers of observation

If you really want to accelerate your networking skills, become a 'people watcher'. Watch body language and how people walk, how they stand, their level of comfort, etc.

- Watch how others work a room.
- Watch how others move around people.
- Note that some people seem invisible and others attract attention.
- Who is warming to who?
- How do people move the energy around the room?
- When someone takes leave of another person, watch the reactions of the person they just left.

What to do if you are tall or short

Michael Vincent, world-class magician, once said to me *'never confuse height with stature'*. Regardless of your physical height and frame, stand correctly.

If taller than the other person:

- Angle your head towards him or her.
- Relax the body slightly but stay upright.
- Talk towards the person, downwards.

If shorter than the other person:

- Take a step back
- Speak clearly, and
- Don't look away too often.
- Talk upwards, towards the person.

The importance of your values and beliefs

It is difficult to keep this section short so I do recommend further reading on this subject. It is very important, however, that you understand that the reason why some people are so good at connecting with others is that they find people who share their values. In this way networking becomes very quick and easy. Let me quickly define for you what I mean by a value. A value is fundamentally what is most important to you. The reason why it is so important is that your values condition your attitude to others. Likewise their values condition their attitude towards you and others.

No matter what your objectives, surround yourself with people who share the same values (and I am not talking about opinions). If you don't have this as common ground these contacts will fall away in time.

- Your values and beliefs differentiate you from other people.
- What is possible/impossible comes from your own thinking.
- This thinking forms your beliefs/values.
- You can only become what you think you can become.
- So you can only experience that which you think you are.

The art of making a really BIG impression

- Practise understanding your body language
- Practise the skill of asking questions
- Practise the art of listening and reflecting
- Practise saying what you think
- Practise sharing your ideas
- Practise taking risks
- Practise asking for what you want
- Practise getting braver
- Practise being who you want to be – step into that role now
- Practise concentrating on the other person and making it interesting for both of you.

About Heather White

Heather White, Founder and CEO of The Magic of Networking Ltd is a networking architect, speaker and author specialising in teaching the skills, behaviours and strategies of professional networking.

Heather's skill is understanding, translating and simplifying the art and science of networking. It is Heather's personal story that helps audiences 'trust' her advice. Moving to London in 1998 she had no contacts, no job and no money - only a business card to check out a networking organisation. She established her first consultancy in 1998 with no commercial experience or role models. And yes it did fail.

It was this lack of initial success that motivated Heather to learn about the power of networking. She attended every networking event she could to learn and practice. And she got really good – so much so she was invited to train others. Magic of Networking was formed in 2001 to meet that need and year on year has grown into its own success story. Today 100% of her business comes from networking and word-of-mouth marketing. This distilled wisdom is what audiences receive.

About the Magic of Networking

The Magic of Networking is a leading specialist in business-to-business relationship development programmes. We deliver a unique blend of consultancy, training and coaching services to align individual personality traits and communication styles with business and career objectives.

We focus on three key elements of networking:

- Developing networking skills, behaviours and strategies for both individuals and teams;
- Creating business opportunities for organisations by building meaningful relationship programmes;
- Finding mentors for senior executives using our extensive network of contacts.

Organisations buy Magic's skills and expertise to resolve issues such as networking for new business, career development, community and personal profiling, soft skills development, internal and external networking and building partnerships.

Magic clients include: BT, Citigroup, Ernst & Young, Lloyds TSB, Metropolitan Police Service, Oracle, Proctor & Gamble, Royal Mint, Allied Irish Bank, Business Link, Clydesdale Bank, The Chartered Institute of Marketing, The Chartered Institute of Personnel and Development, , London Chamber of Commerce & Industry, Royal Mail, Whitehall & Industry Group.

To find out more, please visit:
www.magicofnetworking.co.uk

Testimonials

Rarely have I seen such enthusiasm and it was obvious that people were keen to try out their new found techniques.'

Ceridwen Barkley, Marketing Manager, Allwoods Chartered Accountants and Events coordinator for Professional Women at Lunch (P.R.O.W.L)

'I can't thank Heather enough for the guidance and advice you gave me. As you know I have been trying to formulate my networking approach so that I'm targeting specific industries and people. Your guidance has been invaluable in getting this formulation clear. I now feel that I'll be working smarter and not just harder.'

D'Arcy C.F. Myers, Chief Executive, Dreams Come True Charity

'Heather is outstanding! Thank you very much for sharing your amazing knowledge of how to network with us. The way that you managed to pack so many valuable techniques, tips and practical examples into just one hour was one of the most impressive presentations I have ever experienced. It truly is a "work of art" to see you in action.'

Peter Davey, Chartered Institute of Marketing

'An extremely successful couple of days and an overall satisfaction rate of 85% for Heather's specific workshop - which is fantastic.'

Fergus Lawson, Leadership Unit, Metropolitan Police Service

'I plan to recommend this to colleagues and to our Training Department.'

Lynne Tew, MoD

'... enjoyable and informative...'

Umesh Parekh, Unilever

'... enlightening and extremely useful ..."

Jan Teahon, Kings College Hospital

'Many, many thanks for giving us such a great insight into the power of networking. In addition, there was plenty for everyone to take away from the session.'

Sheree Whatley, FD Swissre,
Chairman of Women's Executive Forum

Testimonials